Charles Joseph Colton, Henry Rightor

Volume of various verse

Charles Joseph Colton, Henry Rightor

Volume of various verse

ISBN/EAN: 9783337124526

Printed in Europe, USA, Canada, Australia, Japan

Cover: Foto ©Thomas Meinert / pixelio.de

More available books at **www.hansebooks.com**

VOLUME

OF

VARIOUS VERSE,

BY

CHARLES J. COLTON.

NEW ORLEANS,
PRESS OF SEARCY & PFAFF,
1899.

TO MY WIFE,
My tenderest, truest, and most constant friend,
This book is,
With fondest affection,
Primarily Inscribed.

Secondary Inscription:
To the New Orleans Press Club.

Introduction.

A certain gratitude is due those who contribute to our amusement and, for all the human wisdom to the contrary, there is as much real good to those old bones of early kings, rotting in tombs and crumbling in mausoleums, from the merry pranks of the jester whose imaginings gave them pleasure, as from the flattery of their courtiers, the advice of their ministers, or the reports of their tax collectors. It is still undecided whether life is worth the living, and will continue to be so until disease and human infirmities have ceased to be part of our lives. In the meanwhile let us be grateful to those who amuse us, who lighten our cares, whose genial imaginings illuminate our dark moments with their sanguine light.

The name of Charles J. Colton, subscribed to verses in various newspapers of this country, notably in the New Orleans Times-Democrat of Mr. Page M. Baker, has, for a number of years, attracted the widest attention and furnished to a great body of readers the most genuine enjoyment. That these verses have struck the popular chord is attested by the extent to which they have been reproduced. Bridget, bringing in the early breakfast, has been equally careful to bring in the morning paper, and, like as not, the first thing turned to was the head of the "All Sorts" column wherein most of the shorter verses have appeared, and where the searcher might be sure to find some whimsical fancy dancing to the lilting measure our poet knows so well.

That man who may speak to the people in the language they understand,—singing to them sweetly and simply and true,—turning the world over and over, smiling at this, laughing at that, lulling tenderly this theme and pathetically that—investing the whole, strange inconceivable mystery of life, its commonplaces and its ideals, with the pleasant color of a gentle, honest mind—that man is far on the road towards poetry as it is measured in the hearts of men and women. Such is Charles J. Colton—and would that you all knew him as this friend does, feeling the warm currents of his simple, boyish, joyous, optimist nature;—such is Charles J. Colton, and may the Fates rock him tenderly for all the pleasure his verses have brought to our world-worn hearts and weary brains!

HENRY RIGHTOR.

Run of Rhymes.

WHAT WE WROTE WHEN WE WANTED TO BE WITTY.

SOME SELECTIONS SUPPOSEDLY SENTIMENTAL.

JUVENILITIES AND GENERALITIES.

What We Wrote When We Wanted to be Witty.

❖ ❖ ❖ ❖

A VALENTINE FOR MY WIFE.

"Oh, what shall I send you, my own dearest love,
  In the shape of a fair valentine?
A card in the form of a carrier dove,
  Bearing love from my heart unto thine?
Or a picture of daisies hid in the green field?
  Or a Cupid who roses does strew?
What token of homage and love shall I yield
  On St. Valentine's day, dear, to you?"

'Twas thus that I wrote, in my office retreat,
  To my sweetfaced and meek little spouse;
The letter completed, a messenger fleet
  Was sent with it up to my house,
And soon did the answering note greet my eye,
  For swiftly the messenger sped;
And when I'd torn open my wifie's reply,
  These words on the paper I read:

"Oh, send me not, loved one, a flowery card,
  Nor one in the shape of a dove,
With silly verse writ by an embryo bard;
  But send, as a token of love,
A little green slip seven inches in length
  By three inches wide, I suppose,
The little slip backed by the government's strength,
  Which an 'X' in its each corner shows."

1

TO LINDAMIRA.

My Lindamira me doth charge
   Something to her to write,
So as to show the world at large
   That I'm her favored knight;
Here is her note: " 'Tis all the mode;
   O loved one, write to me,
A sonnet, eülogy, or ode,
   Or an apostrophe."

Ah, darling girl, didst thou but mind
   How fervently I sweat
(Or perspire, to be more refined)
   O'er every line I get,
Didst thou but know how many a time
   I fret and sigh and sob
In efforts vain to make a rhyme,
   Thou'dst know 'twas no soft job.

And, love, too well I know my muse
   And her forbidding brow,
To think she'll let me air my views
   In verse about thee now;
Besides, the charms that thee bedight,
   Those cherry lips of thine,
Those rosy cheeks, those eyes so bright,
   Need softer pen than mine.

And so, fair one, I must say no
   To part of thy request,
To write, in rhymes of rhythmic flow,
   A verse to thee addressed;
But though your beauties I can't tell
   In ode or elegy,
If apostrophe will do as well,
   Why, darling, here it be: '.

HOW IT WAS FIGURED OUT.

Bob thought his Jane the fairest she beneath the heaven's sun,
And how intensely glad he'd be when once her love he'd 1.

Her hair was of a golden shade, her eyes were soft and blue;
And though quite a coquettish maid, yet she loved Robert, 2.

He vowed that though of girls he'd met in his life quite 3-score,
Until he'd seen his little pet, he'd never loved be-4.

Cried he, "If 5 won your heart, O, sweet love, relieve the pain,
And tell me so in voice whose flow is soft as mu-6 strain."

"The thought is 7 unto me that you will be my mate;
Oh, say not nay, I beg of thee, and my heart lacer-8."

Then smiled on him this maid be-9, and to his prayer replied:
"My love's as 10-der, Bob, as thine; and I will be thy bride."

CURIOUS.

A woman 's a curious creature,
    And it's awkward to size her up right—
Tell her she's chic, and she's happy;
    Call her a hen, and she'll fight.

LOOKING BACKWARD.

Mon Dieu! Mais, le temps, how he fly
   Seence I sing le chanson wiz Marie!
En' I long for zem days zat go by
   W'en she was ma reine, ma cherie.
Ah, zen eet was grand, sapristi!
   Zem days je n'oublierai jamais,
W'en I was un grenadier, me,
   En Marie was een ze ballet.

Zen life was so charmant en bright,
   Lak ze light een ma Marie's belles yeux,
Wiz ze dance een ze ballet at night,
   En zen petit souper pour deux,
Wiz ze vin from ze land of Bordeaux,
   En ze mallard un peu faisande,
W'en I was ze elegant beau,
   En Marie was een ze ballet.

Morbleu! mais zat Fodder Time, he
   N'est pas fair een ze years w'at he bring;
He seem fo' stand still fo' Marie,
   While pour moi he pass by on ze wing.
Je suis a present un grandpere,
   Wiz hair zat fo' long time bin gray,
W'ile Marie's still jolie en fair,
   En ees still dancin' een ze ballet.

HEAVY.

"Cast thy bread upon the water,
   And it will return to thee!"
Well, the sad reflection sorter
   Comes with solid force to me,
If our Irish meal-contriver
   Should obey the proverb plain,
She would have to hire a diver
   Ere she got her bread again.

4

AFTER THE CITY CHAP'S VACATION.

Ye haint hev acted right, Sal, ye've did me orful bad;
My bosom wunst was light, Sal, but ye hev made it sad;
Thet feller come from town, Sal, ez slick ez he could be,
An' w'ile he was aroun', Sal, ye didn't look at me.

Ye used ter take er walk, Sal, 'ith him mos' every night,
An' in his gushin' talk, Sal, ye seemed ter fin' delight;
Ye let him squeeze yer han', Sal, an' let him call ye
    "dear;"
I was er lonesome man, Sal, 'slong's he was here.

He tol' ye he was rich, Sal, but he's jes' got ernough
Ter buy cigars an' sich, Sal, an' it was all er bluff.
Ye was like pie ter him, Sal; ter me ye acted rude,
Ye didn't keer fer Jim, Sal, 'slong's ye had th' dude.

An' now thet he hez gone, Sal, ye're doin' all ye kin,
An' jes' erputtin' on, Sal, ter git me back ergin;
But I tell ye at th' start, Sal, ye made me feel so sore,
I got er noo sweetheart, Sal, an' don't love ye no more.

It hain't no use ter cry, Sal; it mus' be on'erstood,
No matter how ye try, Sal, I'm done 'ith ye fer good;
Th' way ye treated me, Sal, I never kin fergit,
An' ez purty ez ye be, Sal, I don't love ye er bit.

A SOUL-FELT WISH.

Oft in the still and solemn night,
    When sudden waked from peaceful snore,
And when I step, with all my might,
    On tacks a-strewn upon the floor,
Then to my aching heart there does
    An earnest but too vain wish roll,
That I a corporation was,
    And, like it, didn't have a sole.

A LOVE LETTER.

My Love—
     Say my caress you'll meet,
  And I'll sing of thee in flowing meter;
And though my board bill I must beat
  To do so, we'll go to Abita.
My Christian name learn to repeat,
  And in words much hotter than saltpeter,
I'll verses write thine eyes to greet—
  My love, my own, my fair Marg'rita.

Unto no Madeline or Kate
  Will ever I, my darling, cater;
For I have not that awful trait
  That makes of man sometimes a traitor.
Thou, love, shalt be my only mate;
  I swear it by my Alma Mater!
And though we live in direst strait,
  No course than mine could e'er be straighter.

Of graces that do thee bedight,
  I'll ever be the proud inditer.
I'll strive my best to do what's right,
  If need be I'll become a writer;
And if that fails, with all my might
  I'll turn and be a dynamiter,
Or drive a car from morn to night,
  Or leach the desert sands for niter.

I'll never wander from thy side,
  In taverns to swill ale or cider,
And though by other men I'm guyed,
  My wife shall ever be my guider.
Ne'er further from thee I'll be spied
  Than from his web the honest spider.
My wife'll ne'er kick, in life's broad tide,
  'Gainst him to whom the fates have tied her.

6

Oh! love, I'm such a jealous dolt,
    I envy smiles you give Will Dolton;
And oft I wish a thunderbolt
    Would strike that grinning ass, Jim Bolton;
And as for silly Tommy Holt,
    If that same dude I had a holt on,
I'd kill him with my trusty Colt;
    So jealous is

                    Yours,

                        CHARLES J. COLTON.

HANDICAPPED.

Thine eyes are of the bluest blue;
    Thy lips are red and sweet;
Thy two cheeks have the rose's hue;
    Thy figure's plump and neat;
Thy nose is just the dearest nose;
    Thine ears are pink and wee,
And thou'rt, from forehead down to toes,
    As charming as can be.

But yet, with all that thou hast got,
    That form and face divine,
Thou still hast such a saddened lot,
    It grieves this heart of mine;
For Fate—I say it to her shame—
    Thy glowing sky befogs
In giving to thee such a name
    As Maria Polly Boggs.

A WISH FULFILLED.

I sing you a song of a maid named Maria,
Who vowed that no man to her hand should aspire,
Save one who was gifted, whose wishes rose higher
Than to doze through this life at his cottage home fire.
The man whom to wed did this maiden desire,
The loftier subjects of lore must admire,
She cared not for pleasures that riches might buy her,
Her husband might none of this world's goods acquire,
But of high, noble thoughts must his brain be the sire,
And he must rise above the gross earth's lowly mire.

And the truth rippling comes o'er the strings of my
       lyre,
That the maid's wish was carried out fully, entire;
For she did wed a man who rose very much higher
Than the earth, and this fellow's last name was
       O'Dwyer;
The owner he was of a new-patent flyer,
An air machine called, but his fate it was dire,
For he went up one day to a church's high spire,
Jumped off—the machine failed to work, and Maria
Is widowed, and now a new hub does require.

ALPHABETICAL PREFERENCES.

The graduate from high school has his S. A., as we see;
The bankrupt debtor has his O, the old maid sticks
       to T;
The antiquarian likes D. K., the Indian loves T. P.,
The man who doesn't care to work likes something
       that's E. Z.;
The sharper dearly loves the J, the bard loves L. E. G.,
(En passant, so do baldhead men); the sailor sticks to
       C;
The parson's fond of W, because it brings a fee;
And men who're stout are much inclined unto O.B.C.T.

IN THE GARISH GLOAMING.

There's a murmuring noise in the soundless hush,
Where the sleeping kine travel the lea,
    And the motionless river rolls on with a rush
To the placid and billowy sea,
    And the voice of the nightingale cryeth aloud,
In a silent and speechless refrain,
    While the sun smiles down through an opaque cloud,
At the corn on the sterile plain.

There's a breathless calm on the mighty sea,
While the waves rear mountain-high,
    And the bright stars twinkle so merrily
From the darkened and tenebrous sky,
    And the whistle and roar of the chill summer breeze
Melts the ice as it forms on the spar,
    As the good ship ploughs through the turbulent seas,
While she lies fast aground on the bar.

There's a darkling light on the mountain dome,
High-crowned by its peaceful vale,
    While the hydra-headed acephali roam
Adown the precipitous dale;
    And the torrent flows at a snail-like pace,
While the ponderous elves around
    Flit about with a wonderful inert grace,
Where the seaweed flecks the ground.

A PROVERB PROVED.

She grabbed her aching toe in awful anguish,
    And almost cursed the day that she was born;
"Well said," she cried in tones of tensest torture,
    "Hell hath no fury like a woman's corn."

AN APOLOGY FOR THE FOURTH OF JULY.

Dear Lords:
>   Upon our bended knee, while all around, the rabble
> Are shouting out for "Liberty," and such like vulgar babble,
> We ask of thee, with downcast brow, for pity's sake, don't blame us
> For the men who raised that ancient row, and whom the mob call famous.

> Our fathers did, in that dark time, some things they hadn't oughter;
> They slew your sires—O dreadful crime!—and shed their blood like water;
> They made your King a laughing stock; they licked your troops like thunder;
> At Clinton and Burgoyne did mock, and made Lord Howe knock under.

> But, dearest Lords, 'twas not our fault, and had we then been living,
> We would have brought them to a halt, and made them ask forgiving;
> We would have made them pay the tax; 'twere best to make a waiver
> Of so-called rights, than do such acts, and lose your Lordships' favor.

> And we have tried so hard since then to show regret and sorrow
> For the sins of those misguided men: from you our styles we borrow;
> We ape your ties in fond delight, in pants you set our fashion;
> And to worship all that's English quite, is e'er our ruling passion.

No matter what your past may be, when you come o'er
    the waters,
We're always glad to give to thee the pick of our fair
    daughters;
We're proud of honors thus they get, and reck not how
    you treat 'em;
We send our yachts across and let His Royal Highness
    beat 'em.

And therefore, Lords, we ask of you, in bassos and in
    trebles,
Don't visit on our faithful few the crimes of those old
    rebels;
Rest quite assured it gives us pain—this traitorous ju-
    bilation,
And with great reverence,
                 We remain,
                 THE SNOBS' ASSOCIATION.

AN EASTER CAROL.

T his purse of mine, that oft of old
    E nclosed, I vow,
H uge sums of greenbacks and of gold,
    R esembles now
A pancake made in early morn
    B y cook sedate,
T he master's gaze to feast upon
    O n breakfast plate.

E gad! You want to know just why
    N ow it's so flat,
A nd wherefore is it that I sigh—
    N o secret, that!
S can closely these few lines of verse;
    E xpounded there,
T he cause you'll find of this slim purse,
    T his worried air.

11

A BUSTED DREAM.

Morbleu! how I lofe zat sem maiden,
  Ze faires' h'of creature' fo' me,
En I long fo' zat place zey call Aiden,
  W'ere she en I h'only would be;
I have one beeg fuss wiz ze fodder,
  En aussi la mere h'of Estelle,
'Cause wiz her no mo', me, I bodder,
  Seence I meet wiz zat charmante damsel.

Her face eet mek jaloux ze roses;
  Ses yeux lak ze star' have ze shine;
She have ze mos' joli h'of noses,
  En her shep eet be mo' zan divine.
Her teet' zey be w'ite lak ze pearl in
  Ze h'oyster; her hair eet be belle;
No wondair ma tete eet go whirlin',
  W'en I look h'at zat charmante dams

I go to chez lui h'every night wiz
  Some vairy fine cadeau fo' her;
I feel ze whole worl' I will fight wiz,
  Fo' one glance h'of her glorious yeux;
I call her my queen en my daisy,
  En so deep een lofe wiz her I fell,
Mon ami Armant call me crazy
  Wiz regar' to zat charmante damsel.

Mais, now I be no mo' her lover,
  En ze coeur een my breas' eet be triste,
'Cause, helas! me, one day I discover
  Zat zem fine teet' come from ze dentiste,
Zat her shep eet be made up by section,
  En zem locks zey be pairchase' as well,
En h'even zat rosy complexion
  Don't belong to zat charmante damsel.

En w'en mon coeur git h'over breakin',
   R-right stret back to Estelle I go,
En tell her zat I be meestaken,
   En h'aint go'n' do eet h'any mo',
En now, w'en to mon ami Armant,
   H'about zat sem maiden I tell,
I nevair do use zat word "charmante,"
   But seemply call her one dam sell.

POSITIONS REVERSED.

She was a sweet typewriter girl, with eyes of blue,
With tresses just inclined to curl, of golden hue;
When first I saw this maiden fair, her manner meek
Caused me to hire her then and there, at ten per week.

Her spelling wasn't up-to-date; her shorthand skill
Was small; in art of punctuate, her lore was nil;
But she had such a lovely hand and wrist to mate,
I loved to sit down by her and to her dictate.

What though she knew naught of her art; her face was
   kind,
And fault I never had the heart with her to find;
Though she would make, from want of sense, quite
   many breaks,
One gracious smile would recompense her sad mistakes.

One evening (and confound the same!) my fate I tried,
And asked her would she take my name and be my
   bride,
Now I my headstrong folly rue—O cruel fates!
For she I once dictated to, to me dictates.

13

KATE.

Oh, Katie is the sweetest girl
   Upon this earth below;
Her golden hair is all a-curl,
   Her eyes are all aglow;
Her lovely form is rather stout;
   One sixty is her weight,
From which the fact you'll reason out
   That she's no deli-Kate.

Her lovers—she has twenty, at
   The least—in plaintive tone,
Write her so many verses, that
   As dedi-Kate she's known.
She has a humor caustic, dry,
   That nothing can abate;
In fact, so dry is she that I
   Call her my dessi-Kate.

She's just as learned as can be;
   I've oft heard it affirmed
By those who know her well, that she
   Might edu-Kate be termed.
My love for her is fervent as
   That of which poets prate,
And the throne that in my heart she has,
   She'll never abdi-Kate.

She's woven round me such a charm
   I'm sure that never I
Could extri-Kate myself therefrom,
   No matter how I'd try.
Her slightest word is law to me,
   And so I'm forced to state,
Since I'm her abject subject, she
   Must be my predi-Kate.

The charms that did in Venus meet,
　Which Paris deemed the best,
Were not more perfect and complete
　Than those by Kate possessed.
And though you might search every spot,
　And ne'er your quest abate,
You'd find this world of ours does not
　Contain her dupli-Kate.

HOME FROM THE CARD PARTY.

While coming home,
　In awful plight,
This witching hour
　Twixt day and night,
'Tis very strange
　And sad to see
How nature does
　Agree with me.

I'm pretty blue;
　Blue are the skies—
The stars are out;
　I'm "out," likewise;
The moon is full;
　I can't deny,
Although I would,
　That full am I.

The day just broke;
　I must confess,
I'm just broke, too,
　Oh, bitterness!
Just blooming full
　The roses grow;
A blooming fool
　Am I, also.

15

A KITCHEN FREE-FOR-ALL.

The fork said the corkscrew was crooked;
  The remark made the flatiron sad;
The steel knife at once lost its temper,
  And called the teaholder a cad.
The tablespoon stood on its mettle;
  The kettle exhibited bile;
The stove grew hot at the discussion,
  But the ice remained cool all the while.

The way that the cabbage and lettuce
  Kept their heads, was a something sublime;
The greens dared the soup to mix with them,
  And the latter, while it hadn't much thyme,
Got so mad it boiled over; the fire
  Felt put out, and started to cry;
The oven then roasted the turkey,
  And the cook gave the greasespot the lye.

The plate said the clock in the corner
  Transacted its business on tick,
And the plate, which for years had been battered,
  The clock said was full of old nick.
The salt said the cream should be whipped;
  The cinnamon laughed—in a rage,
The cream said the salt was too fresh,
  And it's friend wasn't thought to be sage.

Next the pepper, whose humor is spicy,
  "I dare any fellow," did cry,
"To caster reflection upon me"—
  The mirror took up the defi.
Then the ax, with a wit sharp and cutting,
  Declared that the rug had the floor,
While the key said the knob should be worshiped,
  'Cause it was the right thing to adore.

The bell, ringing in, said the cookbook
  Must be bashful, else wherefore so read?
The stovebrush, a thing of some polish,
  Looked down on the saucer and said
It thought that the same was too shallow,
  But admitted the cup was quite deep;
The coffee tried to climb on the tealeaves,
  But discovered the same were too steep.

You'd not think a thing that's so holey
  As the sieve, would have mixed in the fuss,
But it did, for it said that the butter
  Was a slippery sort of a cuss.
No one knows how the row would have ended,
  Had not the cook, Maggie O'Dowd,
Her work being done, closed the kitchen,
  And thusly shut up the whole crowd.

NO MORE WAKEFUL NIGHTS.

Suffering mankind now should bless me night and
    morning on their knees,
For I've found a cure unfailing for that terrible disease
Known to doctors as insomnia; which keeps folks
    awake at night,
Makes scores of victims crazy and turns darkest hair
    to white.
And I trade not on misfortune, like some others I might
    name,
So I treat all patients gratis, charging nothing for the
    same,
And I tell all those who suffer (let the unbelievers
    scoff)
That the way to cure insomnia, is to
                                sleep
                                    it
                                        off.

17

(The following lines were written by the author of
this book, and delivered by the Hon. Chas. H. Laville-
beuvre, Assistant City Attorney, at the dinner of the
Bar Association of New Orleans, given in July, 1898,
the verses being in response to the toast, "Lawyers'
Liability for a License Tax.")

Mr. Toastmaster :—
I'm quite at a loss to know what to say
On the subject of taxes that lawyers must pay,
And whatever I do say, in making reply,
Is speculative alone, for the fact is, sir, I
Have found that the fellows who follow the biz
Of attorneys, when they learn how easy it is
To evade a debt's payment, and how can be delayed
Liquidation of bills that by rights should be paid,
They into the habit with eagerness fall,
Of not paying any obligations at all.

And as to a license—when a man will refuse
To square up with the cobbler who makes him his shoes,
With the tailor who fashions his coat and his vest,
With the hatman, the shirtman, and all of the rest—
I say, sir, when such bills as these he turns down,
Do you think he'll contribute a tax to the town?
If you do so think, you're very innocent, or
You don't know the average attorney-at-law.

Now, sir, there are men who've been my friends for
    years,
And whose sad plight to-day moves me almost to tears;
Take Smith—ere I captured my job at the Hall,
How often at my humble office he'd call,
And to stir up my envious feelings, would say
That he'd made a fine fee of two fifty that day,
That his earnings that month were twelve hundred
    about,
And he'd make ten thousand cold ere the year petered
    out!

Sir, I envied that man every night, every day,
As I dwelt on the fat fees that floated his way;
But how has he fallen! Since charged I have been
With the job of collecting the licenses in,
With infinite pity for him my heart beats;
The license is based on the annual receipts,
And I find by Smith's statement (please pardon this
    tear)
That the poor fellow made but two hundred last year.

And Jones; sir, alas! he's no longer my friend;
A notice to him the law forced me to send
To come to the Hall and his license to pay,
And he called on me, and, in a furious way,
Demanded to know, since those gentlemen who
The noble profession of burglars pursue,
Since those others who stand on the lonely highway,
And "Your money or life!" so insistently say—
Since they paid of license not one single dime,
Why should we tax lawyers, their brothers in crime?

And because I could not make him understand, sir,
That while lawyers and burglars and highwaymen were
Of a class, yet the former alone had to pay,
'Cause their work's done in a respectable way,
Making forced contributions take the shape of a fee,
His friendship forever has vanished from me—
And these two, the fact your perceptions will reach,
Are by no means the only small rocks on the beach.

And now, in conclusion, I've one word to say:
I hope the millennium will soon come our way,
When lawyers will willingly to the Hall go,
And pay up the taxes they legally owe;
I say, sir, I hope that the day'll come to us
When lawyers will pay, without quarrel or fuss,
Their licenses unto the city—but, still,
I really don't think that the day ever will.

IN SPORTING PHRASE.

Two girls I make my devoirs to,
   And both are truly "out of sight;"
One's curls are of a golden hue,
   The other's locks are black as night;
Yet neither maiden's head of hair
   Than t'other's has of beauty more;
And so between these maidens fair,
   I cannot choose upon that score.

Belle's eyes are just as black as jet,
   While Nellie's are of Heaven's blue;
Yet both so beautiful are that
   One can't decide between the two.
Sweet Nellie's form is plump, petite;
   Belle's slender as the lily's stem;
Yet both so perfect and complete,
   I equally admire them.

Each maiden has a pleasant voice;
   They both have small and well formed ears;
And as to age there is no choice,
   Because they are of equal years;
They both have lips of reddest red,
   And each has teeth of dazzling white;
So that, on either of these heads
   To choose, am I in worried plight.

Each one can bring a handsome dot;
   So, on the question of the glue,
It is impossible to know
   How to determine 'twixt the two;
They each come from an ancient race;
   Both move in same society;
So, as to birth or social place,
   There is no room for choice, you see.

But I will marry Nellie; she
    One vantage has in point of mug;
Belle's nose is straight as straight can be,
    While I just idolize a pug,
And that is little Nellie's case—
    And now you'll want to say, I s'pose,
That in the matrimonial race
    Sweet Nellie wins out by a nose.

SARAH.

The one girl in this world to me
    Is a lovely maid named Sarah,
And once you'd see her, you'd agree
    That earth can hold none fairer.
My mad love brings mirth to my friends,
    But I just up and tell 'em
One glance from her a shiver sends
    Adown my Sarah-bellum.

Her eyes are of cerulean hue,
    While golden are her tresses;
With cheeks and lips of reddest hue
    Dame Nature this maid blesses;
Her glance is modest as can be;
    Her figure neat and trim is;
Yes, take her all in all and she
    One of the Sarah-phim is.

And many eves, when from the sky
    The glowing sun is fading,
With lyre beneath my arm, I hie
    To her house, Sarah-nading,
To vow to her that I'll be true,
    And make her pathway sunny,
If with me she will but go through
    The marriage Sarah-mony.

THE LAWYER'S LAMENT.

I love a girl named Margaret, of cold and haughty
    mien,
Upon whose heart I'd like to get, if possible, a lien,
But, ah, alas! whene'er with warm affection I've ad-
    dressed her,
She'd turn the talk to things which form no part of the
    res gestae.

Although round her with ardent court, I nightly am
    revolving,
Of my attachment she makes sport, and threatens its
    dissolving;
I live next to this maid unkind, yet, spite my earnest
    labor,
The wise injunction she won't mind which bids her
    love her neighbor.

I beg of her, with glowing cheek and trembling
    through my tissues,
To come with me and those words speak with which a
    pair join issues,
But with a laugh that paineth me in the spot whereat
    my heart is,
She says she thinks that it would be a misjoinder of
    parties.

Appeals are of the question out; with them there's no
    use fooling;
Nor would writs of error bring about her judgment's
    overruling;
She is the court of last resort; and by no legal fiction
Could I gain from her parents aught, for they've no
    jurisdiction.

One with a less good cause than I might such a suit
    abandon,
But to reverse this maid I'll try, while I've a leg to
    stand on;
I'll still gigantic efforts make, and keep on pegging at
    her,
And her stern "No" I'll not yet take as *res adjudicata.*

GERMAN WISDOM.

Mynherr Wilhelm Sappy married Fraulein Lizzy
    Nappy, a maiden very scrappy, full of fight;
And since then it is related that this pair so badly
    mated, have a fine old row created every night.

All the day long they are busy, are Wilhelm and his
    Lizzy, but at night they'd set you dizzy with their
    tongues;
There'll be curse and crimination in a Dutch accentua-
    tion, till you're lost in admiration of their lungs.

But last night, as they were sitting by the fire. the
    thought went flitting through her mind they'd best
    be quitting all their strife;
And after much reflection on all matters in connection
    with the move, with some affection said the wife:

"Now, Wilhelm, vot I admire is dot dog und cat,
    Maria, dot can sit down py the fire midout a spat;
Dey stay dere nice und kviet, und dey neffer raise a
    riot—now, vy can't ve two try it, yoost like dat?"

"Yaw," said he, in raising ire; "dot same dog und cat,
    Maria, may sit kviet py de fire—dot's all right,
But, mein frau, I dink you bedder yoost to tie dem two
    togedder, like ve are, und den see vedder dey von't
    fight."

23

'CINDA JANE.

De gal dat I'se in lub wid,
  Her name am 'Cinda Jane;
Sometimes she comes to meet me,
  Down by de orchard lane,
But den she sots me jallous,
  As jallous as kin be,
'Cause she says she's gwine to marry
  Anudder man dan me.

Her brow am like de snowflake—
  Hol' on! I takes dat back;
Hit would be like de snowflake,
  If snowflakes jes' was black;
Her lips am like de roses,
  Her eyes like dimon's shine;
Dar aint no gal dat's sweeter dan
  Dat 'Cinda Jane ob mine.

She's de apple ob my eyeball,
  Am dat same 'Cinda Jane.
But de way sometimes she treats me,
  Hit gibs me lots ob pain;
But still I aint erkickin'
  De leas' bit, 'cause, oh my!
Hit's natchal I should suffah
  Wid a 'Cinda in ma eye.

———

GABRIELLE.

I love a maid named Gabrielle,
  A charming girl is she;
But I can't get a chance to tell
  How dear she is to me,
For her tongue wanders so pell mell
  I get no chance to blab
The love I feel for Gab-rielle,
  With the accent on the Gab.

24

SUPPLANTED.

The Encyclopedia Britannica was sad,
  And a feeling of utter despair
Its breast (if books have a breast at all) had,
  Which held no place wontedly there;
"Alas!" sighed each learned and ponderous tome,
  With a frown on its (let us say) brow,
"Since the girl of the house has from Newcomb come
    home,
They'll have no more use for me now."

IN SUMMER.

Great Scott!
Isn't it hot?
Ninety and two in the shadiest spot;
There isn't, I wot,
A more terrible lot
Than to boil in the heat like a crab in the pot.
No money I've got,
Or I'd purchase a yacht,
And fly o'er the seas to some Esquimaux grot,
Or else share the lot
Of the far Hottentot,
Who revels in comfort where clothing is not.
I envy the sot
Guzzling over his bot,
For no man heeds the heat when he's full or half-shot;
And, Oh! for some spot,
In a palace or cot,
Or a hovel, indeed, where the weather's not hot.

FROM THE COAL DEALER.

I never studied law in all my life;
  My desires ne'er did in that direction run—
Yet I'm familiar with both Blackstone and with Coke
  And past master when it comes to Littleton.

A RHAPSODY.

That my dear sweetheart has her faults,
    I'm very frank in stating,
And faults whereof my sad tongue halts
    And stumbles, in relating;
But, though these habits bad of hers
    Are such that I regret them,
To some good points my mind recurs,
    Which doubly do offset them.

I know—I can't deny the fact—
    That she gets full quite often,
And which would from my love detract,
    Did not, my woe to soften,
The glad reflection come that she
    Is straight up and down in manner,
And free and open as can be,
    However you may scan her.

Sometimes she leaves this mortal ground,
    And seems to soar up higher;
Next suddenly is she cast down,
    In straits severe and dire.
They say—some envious scoffers do—
    (There are many in the city)
That she has wheels; alas! 'tis true,
    And therefore, more's the pity.

When some folk try too high to get,
    And look down on her, it'll
Rouse her up and soon, you bet,
    She'll take them down a little;
But then, great kindness she does show,
    For, when her help's enlisted,
Many men she has, I know,
    To rise in life assisted.

And so I love her; from the morn
  Till eve, am I beside her,
For she's alone dependent on
  My helping hand to guide her;
And whatsoe'er her faults may be,
  Her virtues still are greater;
She's always perfect unto me,
  My own dear Ella Vator.

FROM THE ELECTRICIAN.

Let me volt on my prancing Pegasus,
  For I feel I of Byron ampere,
And can sing for the masses and classes
  A song most delightful to hear;
In fact, I feel sure I conduit,
  For I've written off many a rhyme,
Each said, by all critics who knew it,
  To beat ohm, sweet ohm, every time.

Alas! for the hopes I have fostered!
  Pegasus to move does refuse;
I'm burnt out, my circuit's exhausted—
  Oh! wire you obdurate, Muse?
Say, dost thou deny me expression
  In verse that is flowing and pure,
Because I'm not of the profession,
  But am only a poor armature?

A FITTING REWARD.

"The Henglish honors genius hin hevery walk ot life,"
  Said the British cockney, long and lank and slim;
"W'y, we one time 'ad a bobby w'at got back a stolen
    kid
For his parents, hand you know, sir, w'at the Henglish
    people did?
  They named a 'air restorer hafter 'im."

27

SHERLOCK HOLMES' LATEST TRIUMPH.

An unknown had suicided: to find what he'd been
In life, the noted Sherlock Holmes, of course, had been
    called in;
The great detective searched the clothes upon the de-
    funct man,
And in a confident tone his conclusions thus began:

"That this man lived in Providence is patent to my eye;
Men keep mementoes of their homes, and here's a flask
    of R. I.
And late in Philadelphia he sojourned; that's a fact
That's patent; in his pocket is a last year's almanac.

"Deceased was a book agent; note his canvas shoes;
A hunter, too; his pantaloons of duck doth that dis-
    close;
And fisherman; his underwear of net proves that to
    me——"
And all around were thunderstruck at such sagacity.

IN THE LUNATIC ASYLUM.

The two maniacs were grappled in a terrible embrace,
    Each the lifeblood of the other one did seek;
'Twas a fearful sight to see the fierceness on each livid
    face,
    As each sought upon his foe his wrath to wreak.
But the keepers, twelve in number, with many a punch
    and shove,
    Finally did separate this twain so mad;
Then 'twas ascertained the fuss arose from a discus-
    sion of
    The merits of the wheels the fighters had.

MADE A MISTAKE.

I asked her what her name was;
  'Twas at a crowded ball;
I couldn't see where blame was
  Attached to me at all,
And therefore long I wondered,
  With such a worried air,
Why thusly she responded
  To me, "Well, I declare!"

I'd left her in a hurry,
  'Cause she had gotten mad,
And since then lots of worry
  About the thing I've had;
But now I am elated
  To find this maiden fair
To me had simply stated
  Her name was Ida Clare.

———

THE RULING PASSION STRONG AFTER DEATH.

There was a surly cannibal, of disputatious trend,
  Who of obstinacy had the fullest meed;
Of his tribe there was no member he could truly call a
  friend,
  Because with everyone he disagreed;

So finally they slew him and upon him then they
  dined,
  And after they had gotten through their feed,
'Twas no matter of astonishment with all of them to
  find
  That still with everyone he disagreed.

THE GROUND OF THE PROTEST.

Although 'tis not much to my liking,
   This riding a wheel every day,
Yet I kick not because of her biking;
   But her costume's so greatly outre,
In fact, I might say, so immodest,
   That my fruitless objection refers
Not so much to her habit of riding
   As to that riding habit of hers.

IN THE TWILIGHT.

She walked out in the garden fair,
   I followed, she unknowing, and
With rapture gazed on lips, on hair,
   On eyes, on cheek, on lily hand;
And then I spoke, "Sweet Athenaise!"
   She turned, her fair cheek bore a blush;
That is, to use a poker phrase,
   I called her, and she had a flush.

ALL IN HARMONY.

Her lips would for carnations stand;
   Her brow is like the lily;
Her cheeks are blooming roses, and
   Her ears would knock pinks silly;
Yet 'tis but nature's symmetry
   That all these gifts I've chorussed
Belong to her, because, you see,
   Her father is a florist.

GOT BOTH.

He loved a maid with jet-black eyes, and one whose
   orbs were blue;
To give up either charmer he was loth,
But at last he wed a third girl—and, if neighbors' tales
   are true,
His wife's eyes oft partake of colors both.   .

A DIFFERENCE OF OPINION.

My wife says our baby's a wonder
   At talking, but quite *entre nous,*
The one blessed thing that I ever
   Did hear that kid saying was "Goo."
His ma will ask, "Who's mamma's baby?"
   And "Goo" comes the infant's reply;
And she'll vow he's the cunningest creature
   To use the grammatical "I."

Then she'll ask "Where is mama's boy going?"
   There's a "Goo," and in ecstacy she
Calls the fact to my earnest attention
   He said "downstairs," as plain as could be.
And "What is the itty man after?"
   To my ears a "Goo" loudly doth come,
But I don't to my thought give expression,
   For my wife says he surely said "drum."

And again "Is the itty man seepy?"
   Again is the plastic "Goo" sped;
But my wife says she heard very clearly
   From his lips come the utterance "bed."
And when he's tucked under the cover,
   "Goodnight," she'll say, "mama's boy blue;"
And she'll hear him say "goodnight" distinctly,
   Though to my mind he only said "Goo."

ON THE OCEAN.

It was midnight on the waters, there was silence on the
   deep,
And as far around as eye could see, all nature seemed
   to sleep;
Above, billow, no sound was heard, save in the faraway,
Where each whitecapped wave was surging every other,
   "Let us spray."

TOLD THE TRUTH.

After an absence of some years I came back home, and
    Brown
An old-time chum, I ran across, my second day in town.

I shook him warmly by the hand, inquired of his health,
And was truly glad to know that he was well and rolled
    in wealth.

And then I asked of other friends: "How does old
    Ralph Smith stand?"
Brown groaned and sighed: " 'Tis years since he went
    to the spirit land."

"And Boggs, dear, old Tom Boggs, who used to be so
    gay?" I cried.
Again a groan: "Boggs long ago passed to the other
    side."

"Poor Tom!" I said, "I much regret to learn that he's
    no more;
And how is Jenks?"   "Last year," sighed Brown,
    "Jenks sought the Golden shore."

Dismayed by all this havoc 'mongst my friends grim
    Death had wrought,
To drown the sorrow in my breast a nearby bar I
    sought;

And there I met Sol Robinson.   "Hello," I cry in glee;
"I'm glad to see, friend Robinson, that you're still left
    to me."

"What mean you, Charles?" asks Robinson.   "Why,
    Smith is dead," I say,
"And Boggs, and Jenks, and so I'm glad one friend's
    not passed away."

"Dead!" cries he then: "you're off; Smith's in Kentucky, doing fine;
Tom Boggs lives in Algiers; Jenks runs a California mine."

And so I sharped my trusty blade, my pistol put in trim,
Determined Brown should die the death next time I 'countered him.

But cool reflection came to me, and o'er my mind there rolled
Conviction strong that rascal Brown naught but the truth had told.

MALE PREFERENCES.

The lawyer idolizes Sue, the printer has his Em;
  The sexton in the churchyard has his Nell;
The oyster's stuck on Pearl, or, rather Pearl is stuck on him;
  The motorman is very fond of Belle.

The hotel man likes Dinah, and the doctor Chloe Roform;
  The druggist scarce can make a choice between
The sprightly, gay Mag Nesia and the bright Sal Volatile;
  While Meta is the poet's darling queen.

The up-town man likes Rosa Park, the base-ballist has Fan;
  The shoemaker loves Peg, so people say;
The porter loves his Carry, and the author wants his Pen;
  While the oarsman to his Rose will stick alway.

TROUBLE IN THE PARLOR.

Since the row in the kitchen was settled,
    I thought that our home would have peace,
But it looks like from turmoil and trouble
    We are never to have a surcease.
For, hearing a noise in the parlor,
    I went there to seek the wherefore,
And a scene of confusion confronted
    My eyes as I opened the door.

The sofa had said the wall paper
    Was stuck up—the latter, in scorn,
Declared that the sofa was forward
    And ought to be sat down upon.
The chair said the coal in the fireplace
    Was not gratefull—with consummate gall,
The coal turned around on the lambrequin,
    And said 'twasn't tidy at all.

The fender said it was no blower,
    But would surely not stand any bluff;
The floor cried it was a free trader,
    And considered the carpet tacks tough.
The fire-set started to talking,
    The grate said they'd best hold their tongs;
And the ornaments said that the pictures
    (And their artists, too) ought to be hung.

At this the said pictures retorted
    (While the wainscoting seemed to be board)
That if ever, indeed, they were hung up,
    'Twould be of their own will and a cord.
The shutter cried out that it could not
    See why folks were so mean and unkind,
And the shade said no wonder the shutter
    Couldn't see it—'twas known to be blind.

The window, an open young fellow,
    Said the music box was full of airs,
And the curtains, which needed some sewing,
    Were known for their terrible "tears."
The piano declared that the tassel
    Was a fool and always on a string,
And the tassel replied the piano
    Was too high-toned and haughty a thing.

The trees on the banquette, just outside,
    Peeped in through the window and cried
It thought the whole parlor was shady;
    The table in anger replied
It could say something harsh, if it wanted,
    About the trees' verdure, but said
It wouldn't because it was trees on—
    At this point I tremblingly fled.

SHE CERTAINLY HAS A COLLEGE YELL.

There's not a language she can speak,
    Though she's a college maid;
Not English, Latin, French or Greek,
    Yet she's a college maid.
She never heard of grammar, and
    What's history doesn't understand,
No schoolbook has she ever scanned—
    Yet she's a college maid.

You say that if all these things be
    About this college maid,
You're at a loss to know how she
    Can be a college maid;
Well, she's a little babe, you see,
    Who came this morn at half-past three,
And a Newcome girl, it seems to me,
    Must be a college maid.

FROM THE DAD OF THE FASHIONABLE
GIRL.

My erstwhile peace has taken wing;
   My head is bending low,
And daily am I languishing
   Beneath a weight of woe;
My form with care is getting bent;
   I'm sad as sad can be,
Since first my oldest daughter went
                Into so-ci-e-ty.

A pug nose once adorned her phiz;
   It must have flown away,
For now she says that feature is
   Not pug, but retrousse.
Her name, Maria, wouldn't do,
   She changed it to Marie,
In deference to the tony crew
                She calls so-ci-e-ty.

The parties of her one time friends
   Were pretty slick, she'd say;
But those that lately she attends
   Are simply recherche.
Once for potatoes she did care;
   She doesn't now—you see
Those hightoned folks eat pommes-de-terre
                In her so-ci-e-ty.

My habits has she disarranged,
   Despite my earnest kicks,
My dinner hour she has changed
   From two to half-past six;
And till that time I'm bound to wait,
   Though hungry as can be,
For folks must take their dinner late,
                When in so-ci-e-ty.

If I should take my coat off when
   I'm home, she'll me reprove;
That never is done by the men
   That in her circle move.
My pipe, with which I've evenings spent,
   She's ta'en away from me—
Oh, dern the day Maria went
              Into so-ci-e-ty.

TO A DEAD CAT.

So thou art dead, fair, fondest cat!
   Whom more than horse or dog
I loved, because thou wert the best
   In nature's cat-alogue.

No matter what hour I came home,
   Thou never showed'st surprise,
Nor reasons for my being late
   Would'st ever cat-echize.

While, were I wed, my staying out
   Would meet with criticism
From angry spouse, and, I've no doubt,
   Of tears a cat-aclysm.

And now the cat-enation long
   Death breaks twixt thee and me,
And I am left alone to weep
   O'er this cat-astrophe.

So good-bye—since a cat-acomb
   Must hold thy youth and grace,
The motto I'll place o'er thy grave
   Is "Requies-cat in pace."

37

RETRIBUTION.

In the country one day, wandered Jenkins and I,
And Jenkins is gay, with a humor as high
As that possessed by the immediate Mark Twain, or
the recent Bill Nye.

And the jokes that he had that day played on me
Made me just as mad as I ever could be,
And I vowed that with him I'd get even, the very first
chance I could see.

As the sky it grew dark, we discovered a light
In a house; I remarked we'd best stay there all
night—
You see, we had strayed quite a distance, and the town
was far out of our sight.

So we knocked on the door, and it oped right away,
And there stood us before, a regular jay,
In fact, just the kind of a sucker for whom card sharps
and bunco men pray.

In response to a grin, which pervadeth all
Of his mug, we walk in, and my eyes chance to fall
On a chromo (O Lord! what a horror!) defacing the
parlor's white wall.

But I look at the same with a critical eye;
"By the gods!" I exclaim with a rapturous sigh;
"Here's one of the finest old masters, too precious for
money to buy."

Then does Jenkins deny that such is the case;
"Bet you twenty!" I cry, and the money we place
In the hands of that bucolic donkey, looking on with an
asinine face.

"You'll agree," I cry out; "that this picture so fair
Is the farmer's." "No doubt," does that Jenkins
    declare;
"Then, of course," I rejoin; " 'tis a Reuben's"—and my
    senses fled from me just there.

And the old doctor, he, when at last I awoke
Said the blow that struck me, my jaw nearly broke—
But, Lord! who'd have thought that old Jenkins would
    have gotten so mad at a joke!

ACCUMULATED PROOF.

We've got th' fines' baby
W'at ye ever seen in life,
An' ef ye don't b'leeve it,
W'y, jes' go ax my wife.
An' if ye want er further proof
Thet thet air baby are
The' fines' in th' hull hull worl',
W'y jes' ax my wife's mar;
An' if her word haint good enough
Ter prove thet them's th' fac's,
My own mar, baby's gran'mar too,
Is ernother ye kin ax;
An' if ye still haint satisfied
Erbout that kid, that he
Is the fines' baby in the lan',
W'y dern it all, ax me.

A BIKE EPISODE.

He looks with a scowl at the puncture!
    Then proceeds, with a vehement zeal,
First to blow up the fellow who put the tack there,
    Then to blow up the tire on his wheel.

METHOD IN HIS MADNESS.

He denounced the fad of biking with a virulent inten-
   sity,
   And in language most emphatic said it was a burning
      shame,
And he couldn't understand at all the maniacal propen-
   sity
   Of people in these latter days for riding of the same;
He also said that only men of intellectual density
   Would for a moment think of riding daily on a bike;
And women—well, if his girl folks attempted to com-
   mence it, he
   Would cure them of their folly in a way they wouldn't
      like.

He stuck to the same subject with a wonderful vis-
   cosity,
   And would never let it go, if once he got a solid hold;
Good heavens! How I shuddered at the lightning-like
   velocity
   With which the curses came from him whene'er he'd
      start to scold!
So I looked around to discover the wherefore of the
   verbosity
   Regarding those who rode the bike, which so much
      startled me;
And now I know the cause of his adverbial ferocity,
   For I find that he's the president of a street car
      company.

DOMESTIC AMENITIES.

"Man's work is from sun to sun,
But woman's work is never done,"
   Thus quoted Mrs. Prewett;
Her husband loudly laughed, "Ha, ha!
That shows how lazy women are;
   Why don't they go and do it?"

A RESOURCEFUL FELLOW.

A fellow of wondrous resources is Gray:
    During last summer's great heat,
He thought he would stray, one warm, sultry day,
    To a certain sequestered retreat;
While he lay there at ease, along came a tramp
    Who, bestowing a couple of blows
On Gray's head, knocked him out, and proceeded, the
      scamp!
    To steal the best part of his clothes.

And when Gray recovered, he found himself there,
    'Most as bare as was primeval man;
Perhaps you or I would have died of despair,
    But Gray isn't built on that plan;
For the first thought with him was just how he'd get
      out
    Of his fix; his eye happened to note
Some little doves fluttering their mansion about;
    He dispersed them and captured their cote.

The near railroad track furnished him with a tie;
    Just then, by the luckiest chance,
A thirsty canine came languidly by;
    Gray quickly robbed him of his pants.
The anger he felt, as a matter of course,
    Gave to him a choler straightway,
While the two blows he got with such terrible force,
    As a pair of cuffs served Mr. Gray.

He walked on a bit, and a farmhouse drew nigh;
    Some chickens he saw round there, and
He scared them away with the usual cry,
    And, of course there were "shoos" just to hand.
And thusly accoutered, with shoes, coat, and pants,
    Cuffs, collar, and likewise a tie,
With nothing to show he had met with mischance,
    Straight back to the town he did hie.

THE GHOST.

"Do I love thee? Ask the song bird, twittering forth
 his gladsome lay,
If he loves the balmy woodland in the merry month of
 May.

"Do I love thee? Ask the seagull if he loves the
 wavelets' foam;
Ask the eagle, soaring skyward, if he loves his craggy
 home.

"Do I love thee? Ask the mother if she loves her own
 first born;
Ask the lark that carols gayly if he loves the dawning
 morn.

"Do I love thee? Ask the infant if it loves the
 mother's face;
Ask the gently nodding flowers if they love the sun's
 embrace.

"Do I love thee? Not in words, dear, can my love
 expression find;
I but know thou art my world, dear, that each heart
 beat is all thine."

So I wrote the gentle maiden in the days of auld lang
 syne;
'Twas but one of many follies from this foolish pen of
 mine.

And I thought I'd ne'er more see it, till it was, on
 yesterday,
In her suit for breach of promise, filed and marked
 "Exhibit A."

EDUCATIONAL ITEM.

"What are the four seasons?" the teacher inquired;
 Nor to answer the same was young Tom at a loss,
For this is the answer that at her he fired:
 "Pepper, salt, vinegar, Worcestershire sauce."

ANOTHER FROM SHERLOCK HOMES.

The famous vidocq, Sherlock Homes, and I, stood at
    the bar;
I complimented him upon his great success thus far,
Whereat the sleuth assured me, though in accents of
    some pride,
That 'twas simply observation and deduction, well ap-
    plied.
"For instance," he went on, "this crowd coming in the
    door
Are a lot of gentlemen whom I have never seen before;
Yet I'll merely note the drinks they take, and to me will
    stand confessed
Their respective walks and callings." I watched eagerly
    the test.

"Beer," said the first man—whispered Holmes: "An
    undertaker, sure."
The second asked for "port"—said S.: "A sailor,
    simple, pure."
"Punch," called the third—said Sherlock: "He a pugilist
    must be."
"Gin," cried the next—and Holmes declared: "A cotton
    planter he."
"And he" the sleuth went on, about the last one of the
    group,
"Must be a daily paper scribe"—the youth had called:
    "A scoop."
And when I made the inquiry, to Sherlock's great
    delight,
I found that he in every single instance had been right.

TO MEND THE FRACTURE.

Sir John, the eminent surgeon, gazed out upon the sea,
    As he stood there, with a suit of fine blue serge on;
"When the ocean breaks its waves upon the rocky
    shore," said he,
    "I am glad to see that it will have a surge on."

A FEW THINGS ABOUT THE ALPHABET.

A is the craziest letter; 'tis always in-sane—and the worst

Is the B, for you'll find that in bloodshed, the same is forever the first;

Still, C is not very much better; in crime does it every time lead;

And D's just as bad; 'tis always on hand at the beginning and end of the deed.

E from its birth was affluent, and to live in ease never has ceased,

While F is the leader in fashion and the first at a frolic or feast.

G is the foremost in glory, and in gallantry plays the chief role,

While H , unfortunate fellow ! is all of the time in a hole.

In ignorance and filth doth the I live, and remonstrances have no avail

To curb the J's lawbreaking habits, for he always is lying in jail.

K is the first one in kicking; and perhaps it would be just as well

If the L had never existed, for 'tis now in the extreme of h——l.

With M we'd forever lose music, nor would we have money to pay

For pleasure; and unto temptation, without N we would never say "nay."

O is found in all crookedness, and from politics cannot refrain;

And the P must have been a great sinner, for 'tis now in both penance and pain.

Q is a curious creature, and in quarrels doth always appear;

And if it, with R, leader in riots, should depart, 'twould not cause us to tear.

Were it not for the S we'd know nothing of sorrow, or sin, or of shame,

While the T is the bete noir of heroes, for it maketh
   their fame become tame.
U is a hardworking letter; 'tis always in use, as we see,
And the V liveth in every venture, though in vain may
   the enterprise be.
W forever is getting in the way, human temper to vex,
And its follower is "ten"derly cared for, for who
   doesn't worship an "X?"
Y is a singular fellow, for which reason he never is
   Y's,
And the Z, though behind all its brethren, yet cuts quite
   a figure in size.
And thus any curious observer, as he downward from
   A to Z goes,
Will find each particular letter some very strange
   quality shows.

A MISUNDERSTANDING.

I know that I told you "bye-bye," little wife,
   On yester, when up-town you sped;
But greatly I'm fearing, O light of my life!
   That you misconstrued what I said.
For to judge by the bills handed to me to-day
   For things you invested in, I
Feel certain that you, in your innocent way,
   Understood me to tell you "buy, buy."

VERY BRILLIANT.

"Jenkinson's a brilliant man, "said Bluffer;
   And I took issue with him on the spot,
For a peanut shell will cover (and leave lots of room
   left over)
Every grain of sense that Jenkinson has got.
But Bluffer just proceeded on to prove it—
   "What is brilliancy but light?" to me he cried;
And then he tapped his head quite meaningly, and said:
   "And that Jenkinson is light can't be denied."

45

AN OPEN LETTER.

Let me tell you, through the medium of the press, my
    wife,
  What I'd dare not say, if facing you, alone;
That to put aside all prejudice, I guess, my wife,
  There are other babes as pretty as our own.

Now, there's not the slightest use in getting riled, my
    wife,
  (Remember, I'm at present far from thee),
When I say that though I dearly love our child, my
    wife,
  Yet I know some others are as smart as he.

And I cannot longer hold from you the truth, my wife,
  Though I know 'twill likely set you in a rage,
There may have been some kids besides our youth, my
    wife,
  Who weighed just as much as he did, at his age.

As you say, his eyes are bright as any star, my wife,
  And, of course, he no doubt has a charming phiz,
But I'd not wonder if some other babes there are, my
    wife,
  With eyes and faces just as nice as his.

And now that I have had a chance to tell, my wife,
  To you the things I long have wished to say,
Please 'phone me—search your inmost bosom well,
    my wife—
  If you think I'm safe in coming home to-day.

THE TENTH ANNIVERSARY.

"Faith, phot do they call it th' tin widdin' fur?"
Asked Danny McDuff of the Widdy Muldoon;
  And this is the answer that he got from her:
"Bedad, 'cause it's tin years they're married, ye loon!"

THE BOYS THE GIRLS LIKE.

The female gambler dearly loves her Wynne;
The girl who's brokenhearted sticks to Si;
   The athletic maiden ever thinks of Gym,
And the ever-teasing coquette has her Guy.
  The shoplifter fair to Rob would give her hand
The girl who's fond of painting loves her Art;
   While the maid in the Salvation Army's band,
Dotes on her Sam with all her guileless heart.

When the social leader loses all her grace,
Of course it makes her sorrowful, but then,
   Though no longer she's the belle around the place,
She is satisfied to know that she has Ben.
  The Irish peasant woman has her Pete;
Girls fond of diamonds stick to Jem alway;
   E'en the Amazon in Afric's hot retreat
Has her Manuel of arms, explorers say.

The girl who likes to show off Pomp does love:
The woman with a strong mind wants her Will—
   And all the preferences named above
Are shown in ordinary times, but still
  There are also times when for one man alone
Every woman's heart a strong desire does feel;
   For when female stomachs pangs of hunger own,
Then all their thoughts are centered on Emile.

FROM THE ARTIST.

I am so very poor, you know,
  I live up in a garret,
Through which the winter wind doth blow,
  So cold I scarce can bear it.
O'ershadowed is my life with gloom,
  For to me the fact's emphatic,
That living in this attic room
  Will soon make me rheumatic.

WAR AMONG THE BOOKS.

There was a Dickens of a Rowan the library;
  The whole doggoned crowd were incensed
With each other—it scarce needs the stating
  That it all about a woman commenced.
It seems "She" fell out with her Lover,
  But the squabble had caused her such Paine
She began ('tis 'mongst mortals quite different)
  To Sue to be friendly again.

Now he, quite determined to Lever,
  Asked the friend next to him on the shelf
To go and so tell her; the latter
  Replied, "Hugo tell her yourself."
Another book Lytton the gallant,
  And cried, "It's a shame," in a rage;
But the youth said he could not be expected
  To Marryat his tender age.

Some books cried out, "Now, don't you blame him;
  Ouida done the same thing in his place,"
But others said he was too Harte-less,
  And the same was a sin and disgrace.
The youth, seeing well he could never
  Get Scott-free of his troubles out,
Began Irving himself for the struggle
  Which soon would be raging About.

"By my Life," cried out sturdy old Johnson,
  "Were the days of the tournament here,
He'd Rousseau ungallant an action
  As long as this arm could Shakespeare."
The young man at this grew quite Haggard,
  But being Hardy, with a craw full of Sand,
He declared, in a voice Strong and Savage,
  He'd never retreat from his stand.

The fuss had assumed great proportions
　In a way that was pretty D—n Swift,
And the Hope had become Nye exhausted
　That the darkening clouds e'er would lift.
'Twas a Marvel, although, to discover
　Howell a few books had kept still,
Simply saying, "What are all of these Wordsworth?
　They'll never make him change his will."

The maiden here cried, "I'll release him
　If he Burns all my letters"—"But oh!"
From the top Roe called out English Junius,
　"Hume mustn't burn mine, sir, you know."
"Great 'Evans," cried out Chimmie Fadden,
　"Will Hughes fellers git on to de bloke?
Dem letters ain't fit ter Reade, nohow"—
　And poor Junius looked ready to Croke.

Someone said it was well they were parted,
　No peace 'twixt the Twain e'er would be,
For he'd Cooper up, certain as shooting,
　So jealous a fellow was he;
And, of course, such a thing would be very
　Em-Barrie-sing—cried the bookcase, "No More:
This straw breaks the back of the Campbell:"
　Then it groaned and fell down on the floor.

A CHRISTMAS SOLILOQUY.

"Old Santa makes his presence felt about this time of
　　year,"
　And his eyes upon his new tile fondly dwelt;
"For straw hats in December would indeed be rather
　　queer,
　And so the old man makes his presents felt."

49

WOMAN'S WAY.

"Garbess its itty seffy, ze bessed itty sing,
Zare ain't ennuzzer fezzer zat's half as shmart as hing;
Zu putty dumpy lumpy, akutchukutchuku,
Er itty ossymoosy, er googlegooglegoo."

What is it, you ask? A Zululand song?
  You're a poor hand at guessing, in sooth,
Because it is just what I heard my wife say
  When she found that our kid had a tooth.

10-TATIVELY.

I love thee 10-derly, O Kate!
  With love in-10-se and true;
My heart's tree throws a 10-dril out,
  That reaches, dear, to you.
My feelings I do not pre-10-d,
  Nor have I 10-dency
To make my heart so 10-sile as
  To cover more than thee;
10-aciously I cling to thee,
  Nor will I be con-10-t,
Until we two joint 10-ants are
  Of the self-same 10-ement.

A PROVERB DISPROVED.

When the maid who got stuck on the boxer's dexterity,
  By him to the hymeneal altar was brought,
What a fool was the man who declared as a verity
  That feint art ne'er won fair lady! methought.

ADVICE FROM THE SOLDIER.

Whene'er the threat of ravage rude
  To crops doth make the farmers squirm,
They ought to build up Fort Itude
  To check the coming Army Worm.

REPENTANCE.

When I dwell on the crimes I've committed,
  The thought makes me tremble with dread,
I remember once going to Kilpatrick,
  And in racing I once forged ahead.
I once stole a march, playing euchre;
  In the street I have often cut men ;
Many times I went forth, bent on sleighing,
  And have stoned raisins time and again.
In liquor I've often drowned sorrow ;
  I've hung my watch up when in need,
And I once slew a beautiful rooster,
  Which you'll admit was a pretty fowl deed.

ABOUT THE MEDICAL PROFESSION.

Euphemize it as you will, the stern and frigid fact
  remains.
  Though I've no doubt some folks will think it funny :
The wealth of a physician is at best ill-gotten gains,
  And the fortune of a surgeon is bloodmoney.

TO THE POSTER GIRL.

O, poster girl! wert thou my bride,
  Joys would to me ecru ;
I long to have thee by my side,
  Dog-garnet, yes, I do!
Oh, carmine own and fly with me,
  For verily I swear,
Life would be one long dream with thee,
  Or, rather, one nightmare.

Some Selections Supposedly Sentimental.

✧ ✧ ✧ ✧ ✧

TWO FLOWERS.

Only a flower! 'Twas last night a part
  Of the bouquet she wore at her breast.
Only a flower! Yet close to his heart
  With a true lover's passion 'tis pressed.
Only a flower! A pitiful thing!
  Yet dearer than Kohinoor's gem;
For a trace of his loved one seemed fondly to cling,
  Even yet, unto petals and stem.

Only a flower! On yester it grew
  On the grave of a wee little child,
Whom its fond mother knew for a moment or two,
  And then saw it die as it smiled.
Only a flower! Yet priceless its worth,
  Because its brief life had begun
From the handful of earth o'er the babe twixt whose
      birth
  And death, but a moment had run.

Time passes quickly; at last came a day
  When the fond lover carelessly cast
The flower away of his sweetheart's bouquet,
  With a laugh for the dream that was past.
But that other white flower, though withered and sere,
  With petals all fallen apart,
Grows year after year more precious and dear
  To the young mother's sorrowing heart.

A DREAM.

Methought a message to and fro
Across our continent did go,
That brought with it a tale of woe
To rich, to poor, to high, to low;
That forced the tear from Age's eye,
And caused the infant's breast to sigh—
   And this is all the message said:
     "Jim Riley's dead."

Methought I walked into the day;
The skies above were leaden-gray;
The glowing sun had hid away;
The mocker hushed his thrilling lay;
The sturdy oaks were bare and drear;
The meadow grass was dry and sere—
   For hither had the message sped:
     "Jim Riley's dead."

Methought a garden erstwhile fair
I traversed—dahlias withered there;
The violet lost its odor rare;
No more the rose perfumed the air;
The lilies rotted on the stem;
The pansies' hues had flown from them—
   Here, also, was the message read:
     "Jim Riley's dead."

And then I woke—the sun shone down;
I heard the mocker's sweetest sound;
Bright flowers sprang up from the ground;
And all was peace and joy around;
And as upon my dream I dwelt,
I prayed, as reverent I knelt:
   "May not, till many years have sped,
     The message come, 'Jim Riley's dead.'"

RETROSPECTIVELY.

How this bundle of time-worn old letters
  Turns my thoughts to the days that are fled,
When my heart was a captive in fetters
  To lips of the cherriest red,
To eyes like the brightest stars gleaming,
  To cheeks of the rosiest hue,
In those days of love's earliest dreaming,
  When I was but twenty and two.

Adown through a lengthening vista
  I see as these lines I read o'er,
To the soft moonlight night when I kissed her,
  And bade her good-bye at the door;
And swore, by the Heaven above her,
  That the heart in my bosom was true,
That forever and ever I'd love her,
  When I was but twenty and two.

And these letters, all tenderly breathing
  The love of her innocent breast,
To-night seem around me enwreathing
  A spirit of infinite rest;
The years, with whatever of sorrow
  They brought, fade away from the view,
As a few fleeting moments I borrow
  From the time I was twenty and two.

See, here she refers to some verses
  I wrote for her autograph book;
And there a shy sentence rehearses
  The walk that we yesterday took;
And here is a line to awaken
  My mem'ry: "You know, dear, that you
Were to go get your photographs taken"—
  When I was but twenty and two.

Ah, me! It scarce seems that 'tis seven
    Long years since I first read each line,
With the thought that no angel in Heaven
    Had a happier portion than mine;
And I swore, with a fond lover's fervor,
    My dream was too sweet to be true—
For I knew that I didn't deserve her,
    When I was but twenty and two.

Now my wife o'er my shoulder is leaning,
    And yet to my bosom there rise
No thoughts that I'd better be screening
    These letters of old from her eyes;
What care I although she may note them?
    I know that the fact I'll not rue,
For she was the maiden who wrote them,
    When I was but twenty and two.

A CHILD'S GRAVE.

Only a grave where a little child lies,
    Where the headboard says, "Baby, aged two!"
A wee little grave lying under the skies,
    All covered and shrouded with dew!
The smallest of heaps, the tiniest mound,
    Lying there in the shade of the hill,
In the midst of the other graves scattered around
    In the churchyard so silent and still.

But, think ye that only an infant lies there?
    Ah, no! there are other things, too;
There are plans for a future so smiling and fair;
    There are hopes for the years to accrue;
There are visions that now are all banished and fled;
    There are dreams that can never come true;
And the heart of a mother, all joyless and dead,
    Lies also there, under the dew.

THE BACHELOR'S DREAM.

(To Ik Marvel, with thanks for the idea and apologies
for the theft.)

As I sit 'fore my bachelor fireplace
  I dream of a possible life:
Of a dear little oak-bowered cottage,
  Of a sweet-faced and true little wife:
Of a glad coming home in the evening
  To a place where forgotten are cares;
Of a wife's welcome, tender and heartfelt,
  Of a babe at my knee lisping prayers.

(I poke up the fire—it blazes
  And burns with a flame strong and bright).
I gaze on a scene of the future
  In the glow of the coal's ruddy light.
We're seated at eve in the garden;
  My baby rolls 'round in the grass;
My wife with her fancy work by me,
  And the hours in sweet happiness pass.

(Again does the poker its duty;
  The fire does not burn as before;
But alternate lights and grim shadows
  Are cast out upon the bare floor).
And now grim Death's angel is hovering
  O'er our suffering baby's white bed;
The blue eyes are closing so gently,
  And the soul of our darling has fled.

(The light goes down dimmer and dimmer,
  And naught now is left but a spark).
My dear wife is tossing in anguish,
  And the sky of the future grows dark.
I fold the white hands on her bosom,
  I stifle the half-uttered moan:
No tears now—the well is exhausted,
  And my heart is as heavy as stone.

Heigh-ho! all my dreams are but idle;
  Their fruition may Heaven restrain;
(I give a few vigorous pushes,
  And the flames start out brightly again).
A tear! By my word! Why, how foolish!
  And o'er mythical baby and wife;
Ah! no, I don't want my heart broken,
  So I'll stick to my bachelor life.

———

TWO SOVEREIGNS.

My heart's but a divided throne;
  Two queens sit regnant there;
Yet neither cares to rule alone,
  Nor seeks the other's share.
No hatred glooms their lives around;
  They know not envy's pain,
But gentle peace and joy abound
  Beneath their dual reign.

You say that never woman was
  On earth as these so meek,
And wonder much why neither does
  To oust her rival seek.
But it is plain to understand
  Why twixt them there's no strife;
For one's my little daughter, and
  The other is my wife.

EUGENE FIELD.

Lay him down gently—
  Him whose refrain
Spoke eloquently
  Not to the brain,
Not to man's reasoning—
  Mission of Art—
But with love's seasoning,
  Straight to the heart.

Scatter the flowers
  Over the bier
Of him whose hours
  Spent with us here,
Each one succeeding,
  Brought from his pen
Sweetest of pleading—
  Gentlest of men!

Place here his dollies,
  Lassies and lads—
Simplest of follies—
  Mildest of fads—
Here in his coffin,
  Here where he lies,
They who so often
  Gladdened his eyes.

Here but his semblance—still,
  Life-vanished clay;
Here but remembrance will
  Keep him alway.
Voices that spoke in him
  Tremblingly fled
When the heart broke in him,
  Leaving him dead.

Peacefully sleeping,
　　There as he lay,
Azrael, weeping,
　　Bade him away;
Saw he the beckoning,
　　Heard the award;
Gone to his reckoning,
　　Gone to his Lord.

Lay him beneath here,
　　Under the sod;
Twine but a wreath here—
　　Leave him to God.
From scenes terrestrial
　　Gone to his home;
'Mid joys celestial
　　Ever to roam.

YE MAID OF OLDEN TIME.

We see her picture over there,
　　In quaint, old-fashioned dress,
With modest mien and meekest air,
　　A world of tenderness
Within the eyes that seem to glow
　　With innocence sublime;
The girl John Alden used to know,
　　In the old Colonial time.

What though she lacked the *savoir faire*
　　That modern maids possess!
Not one thought would her bosom bear
　　Her lips dared not confess.
And so we sing in deepest praise
　　And reverential rhyme,
Of the maid who cheered the troublous days
　　In the old Colonial time.

THE NINE O'CLOCK BELL.

As I sit here to-night, with the rolling inflections
    Of the city bell tolling the hour of nine,
Falling harsh on my ear, how the fond recollections
    Of boyhood come unto this bosom of mine!
And mem'ry brings to me the market-place meetings,
    Where we urchins all loved to assemble so well,
And to play 'neath its arches till sent homeward fleeting
    By the intoning voice of the nine o'clock bell.

How well I remember each blood-curdling story
    That Moulton would tell us of Buffalo Bill,
Or of wild Deadwood Dick and his career of glory,
    While we gathered round him so awestruck and still!
And how, while the moments unnoticed were slipping,
    There came that dread sound all our dreams to dispel,
And then the mad race, to avoid the sure whipping
    Should we fail to beat homeward the nine o'clock
        bell.

How my musing recalls the parental injunction,
    "Be home, sir, at nine, or I'll wallop you sore;"
And which rule disobeyed brought the direst compunc-
        tion
    When I dwelt on the licking most surely in store;
And oft was it due me, for, under the power
    Of the witching adventures that Moulton would tell,
I'd linger entranced until long past the hour
    Tolled out by the strokes of the nine o'clock bell.

Ah, me! as I sit here in melting and mild mood,
    With my eyelids shut tight and my thoughts back-
        ward cast,
I seem to live o'er the gone days of my childhood,
    Forever dissolved in the mists of the past.
And there comes once again the deep iron-voiced clat-
        ter,
    The crowd of scared urchins dispersing pell mell,
The hurried good-nights and the footsteps' swift patter,
    Beating home the last tap of the nine o'clock bell.

ARCHBISHOP JANSSENS.

There came before the great white throne
    A soul from earth just free;
And God called, in commanding tone:
    "His record bring to Me."

And unto where the King doth sit,
    They brought the book wherein
Each act of man on earth is writ,
    Each good deed, and each sin.

The Eye sought first the credit page;
    O'er Righteousness did scan;
Saw Truth writ there since early age;
    Saw Love of fellow-man;

It gazed on Anger held at bay;
    Marked Charity divine;
Beheld Temptation bidden "nay;"
    And Honor's graven sign.

Saw Piety's unchanging reign;
    Humility discerned;
Marked Fortitude 'neath sorest pain;
    On Faith's inscription turned.

And so on, straight along the page,
    The credit entries ran,
All showing how, on life's broad stage,
    He'd played the perfect man.

And then adown the debit side,
    The judging Vision sank;
There, not an entry it descried—
    For, lo! the page was blank!

WITH AUTUMN'S COMING.

Comes the falltime, with the whirring
   Of the winds among the trees,
And the golden leaflets stirring
   Here and there with every breeze;
And the robin redbreast singing,
   As he circles to the sky,
Seems a hope of blessings bringing,
   Yonder where the orchards lie.

Let us leave the pent-up city,
   With its ceaseless crash and whirl,
And its lack of Christian pity,
   For the place where brooklets purl;
Where the peaceful kine are lowing
   In the meadows sweet and green,
And the flowers wild are growing,
   In fair nature's own demesne.

Let us turn our weary faces
   From the town's incessant fray,
And go seek the pleasant places
   In the country far away,
Where despair is never lurking
   And devouring whom it can;
Where no man's intent on working
   Utter woe to fellow man.

Here, the warfare never waneth
   Twixt oppressor and oppressed;
There, soft peace forever reigneth,
   And the weary are at rest;
Here, the heart is bound with pinions;
   There, the songs of freedom ring;
Here, are mortal man's dominions;
   There, our God alone is King.

Let us, therefore, gladly wander
  To the country fair and green,
There to idly dream and ponder
  In some simple, sylvan scene;
There to live 'neath peace's pennant,
  Till we're laid beneath the sod,
And our frame's immortal tenant
  Seeks a fellowship with God.

———

SPRING.

There's a titillant thrill in the ambient air;
  There's a tremulous tint in the sky;
There's an echo afloat from the haze over there,
  Where the expectant meadowlands lie;
The redolent roses in rapture rejoice,
  The lark loudly lilts upon high,
And even the verecund violet's voice
  Cries out that the springtime is nigh.

There's a rising refrain from the rollicking rill,
  As it rushes its rushes along,
While the sturdier stream seems its soul forth to spill
  In sonorous and satisfied song;
And the winds, as they wantonly wander the wood,
  And through hemlock and holly tree hum,
Seem in mellowest music and merriest mood,
  To tell us that springtime has come.

❖ ❖ ❖ ❖

SCARING PAPA.

Often, when I'm sitting in the quiet eventide,
With a volume from my book case very much preoccu-
    pied,
My baby'll come tiptoeing, till he gets behind my chair,
With the mischief beaming from his eyes; and while
    he's standing there,
Of course, all my attention is concentred on my book,
And it never once occurs to me behind my chair to look,
But I just keep on my reading, till,with wild hullabaloo,
I start up in a great alarm,
                 when
                     baby
                         hollas
                             "Boo!"

And when I ask, in dreadful fear, "Oh my, what can
    that be?"
He'll cry out "Me 'care papa," while he claps his hands
    in glee;
So I make out I'm offended, and he'll come and kiss me
    then,
And tell me, with a roguish smile, he won't scare me
    again;
But no sooner am I seated, with my book again in hand,
Than the cunning little rascal will take up his erstwhile
    stand,
And while I'm trying earnestly my story to pursue,
Once more I'm frightened from my seat,
                 when
                     baby
                         hollas
                             "Boo!"

And in endless repetition we'll enact the self-same
    scenes;
I really don't believe he knows at all what "chestnut"
    means,
For the game he keeps on playing, and repeats it o'er
    and o'er,
And each time my fright is greater than it was the time
    before,
Till at last the blinking eyelids and the little nodding
    head
Betoken that my baby boy is ready for his bed,
So off he goes and leaves me, gladly looking forward to
Another fright to-morrow night,
                when
                    baby
                        hollas
                            "Boo!"

PROOF POSITIVE.

I knew not if baby was sleeping,
    As I bent over him in his bed;
Tight shut his two eyes he was keeping,
    But suspicions were rife in my head;
And I thought by inquiring that maybe
    I'd get him the truth to confess,
So I asked: "Are you fast asleep, baby?"
    And his answer came soft to me, "Yes."

TO LITTLE ETHEL.

Would you go, little girl, to a faraway land,
   Many, many miles over the sea,
Where all that is nice is placed close to our hand,
   And life is as glad as can be?
Where the floors of the houses are made out of pies,
   And the nails are all chocolate creams,
Where the walls are of cake, and the windows like-
     wise—
   In that beautiful country of Dreams.

Oh, the doors are all made out of ice cream, I'm told,
   And the keys out of strawberry tarts;
While the sills are bananas, as yellow as gold,
   And the hinges are peppermint hearts;
And all round about this fair land, I've heard say,
   There are wonderful fountains and streams,
Which flow nothing but nectar and cream the whole
     day—
   In that beautiful country of Dreams.

As for fruits, there are plenty, and all of the best;
   There are cherry trees, apple trees, fig,
And pears and pecans till you really can't rest,
   And melons enormously big;
And of all of these fruits, and these candies and such,
   You can take what you want, for it seems
There never comes sickness from eating too much,
   In that beautiful country of Dreams.

And playthings abound till I'm sure you would think
   There were millions there, lining the shelves;
There are dollies that talk, and dollies that wink,
   And dollies that walk by themselves;
There are dear little buggies to take the dolls out,
   Drawn along by the cutest of teams;
And a whole lot of other toys scattered about
   In that beautiful country of Dreams.

So you'd like to go there, little maiden, you say;
   Well, come here and sit on my knee,
With your soft hand in mine, and your curly head lay
   Right here on my breast, and we'll see
As we rock to and fro in this great big armchair,
   That so cozy and comforting seems,
How long it will take me to carry you there,
   To that beautiful country of Dreams.

THE LAND OF NOD.

Oh, don't you love the land of Nod, my baby,
   Where all the little children go at night,
To wander 'neath the eye of God, my baby,
   In those pleasant realms of ever-new delight?
Where the gentle angels play with thee, my baby,
   And show thee many a soft and beauteous sight,
Until they give thee back to me, my baby,
   When the morning glow has put the shades to flight?

I wonder just what joys are there, my baby,
   That make you smile so often in your sleep!
Are the ones who welcome you so fair, my baby?
   And the pleasures that you drink in, are they deep?
'Tis a pity that you cannot speak, my baby,
   Else would that tongue to me relate the tale
Of the beauties of the land you seek, my baby,
   When sleep across your eyelids throws her veil.

And tell me, through the happy day, my baby,
   When those azure orbs are lit with childish glee,
In the midst of all your romp and play, my baby,
   Does a longing for the nighttime come to thee?
Do you wish the glowing sun would sink, my baby,
   So the horses of the twilight, lightly shod,
Could come for thee when eyelids blink, my baby,
   To bring thee once more to the land of Nod?

TO A DISSATISFIED SCHOOLBOY.

Oh, come, little grumbler, and travel with me,
Over river and valley and prairie and sea,
Over hill, over dale, over mountain of stone,
To a faraway country I know of alone,
    Where there's nothing to worry,
    And fractions don't flurry,
And there's never a lesson to get in a hurry;
Where the sun's ever shining, the sky's ever blue,
And birds ever warble for me and for you,
Where there are no historical dates to recall—
In that wonderful country of Nowhere-at-All.

Come, fly away quickly; the fairies so bright
Are patiently waiting to see us alight
From the beautiful carriage they've placed at our hand,
To carry us off to their mystical land,
    Where nothing will vex us,
    And no one expects us
To spell Yangtsekiang, or bound drear old Texas;
Where there's nothing to do but lie in the grass
And watch the light clouds as they lazily pass,
Or play on the sward with the bat and the ball,
In that wonderful country of Nowhere-at-All.

Come on, let's not linger, for time quickly flies;
In a moment you'll be 'neath the schoolmaster's eyes,
In sound of his voice and in reach of his hand;
Then farewell all thoughts of that wonderful land,
    Where rhetoric won't task us,
    And none care to ask us
The length of the Rhine or the size of Damascus;
Where there's never "Steele's Physics" and hygiene's
    forgot,
And parsing and cube roots are both voted rot;
Come haste, and ere night on the sad earth doth fall,
We'll be safe in the country of Nowhere-at-All.

TO MY BABY BOY.

When my baby's eyes first open
  In the early morning light,
I go to him, and peering
  Down in those orbs so bright,
I ask, "Where's papa's baby?"
  With such a roguish air
His hand will tap his bosom,
  As he answers me,
    "Wight dare."

"Where are the little angels
  That played with you, my boy,
As in your dreams you wandered
  Last night in realms of joy?"
He seems to comprehend me;
  Straight upward in the air
One chubby finger's pointing,
  And the answer comes,
    "Wight dare."

Along on through the daytime,
  When dirt, from head to foot,
Encrusts his form and features,
  The question I will put,
"Where is one clean spot, baby,
  On that face anywhere?"
He points up to his forehead
  And answers me,
    "Wight dare."

And when the years go winging,
  And his time comes to die,
Among the angels singing
  In bliss beyond the sky,
O Ruler of the Heavens
  I beg Thee hear my prayer—
See to it, in Thy goodness,
  That my darling is
    "Wight dare."

BABY'S DAY.

Baby gets up in the morning, with no definite object in
    view.
No thought as to how he'll be spending the hours that
    each other pursue,
For a moment devoted to planning would be useless
    and certainly wrong;
Isn't baby equipped to encounter whatever may happen
    along?

As a start, with his little toy hammer he'll smash in the
    face of the clock,
But the tool by his papa is taken, which gives to his
    pride such a shock
He's about to break out into crying, but hold, there is
    quite as much fun
To be had, he determines, in fooling with the trigger
    of papa's shot gun.

Now, papa, aware of the danger, snatches the weapon
    away;
Baby, annoyed beyond measure, thereon decides he will
    play
At seeing in how many pieces he can tear one of papa's
    pet books;
Again are his efforts frustrated, while his brow wears
    the saddest of looks;

For what can he do, the poor baby, the hours away to
    beguile?
Ha! the inkstand! there's lot's of fun painting the tom-
    cat, he thinks, with a smile;
But Tommy objects to the spoiling of his fur that's so
    shining and smooth,
So the upshot is two or three scratches and some tears
    which dear mama must soothe.

Soon the clouds clear away and the sunshine once more
    decks his rubicund face;
He'll get papa's file full of papers and scatter them over
    the place;
His pride hurt that no one is watching, he wonders if
    breaking the glass
With his ball will attract some attention, which it does,
    to his sorrow, alas!

Again he's his mama's lap seeking, that haven of com-
    fort and rest,
And he sighs out his trials and troubles, with his face to
    her bosom close pressed.
A few words of softest endearment from her, serves to
    banish his pain;
So he wastes time that's precious no longer, but starts
    on his career again.

Ha, he'll drive some nails in the piano, but pa puts a
    stop to the play,
And he thinks, with a glance of resentment, papa's most
    outrageous to-day,
And the frown on his forehead betokens the wrath that
    his bosom doth swell;
And the next time such cruelty happens he determines
    at once to rebel.

But, lord, 8 o'clock now is striking; why, who would
    have thought it so late?
The two little blue eyes are closing, and to bed with the
    wobbliest gait
He goes, to spend hours in sleeping, till the sun doth
    again o'er earth soar;
When he'll wake up refreshed, to go searching around
    for adventures once more.

THAT LITTLE GIRL OF MINE.

As I sit in peaceful quiet, at the closing of the day,
And watch my little daughter with the neighbor's children play,
While my wife sits close beside me, in her basket rocking chair,
And enjoys with me to gaze upon the babies romping there,
I can feel the cares of business from my worried mind depart,
And a glow of glad contentment warms the cockles of my heart,
As I see the curling ringlets and the eyes that brightly shine,
And hear the pealing laughter of that little girl of mine.

What a ruddy, healthy color to her cheek her playing brings!
Now she starts a recitation or a snatch of song she sings
In the little childish treble that to me has sweeter grown
Than the melody of Nilsson or the Patti's soaring tone.
What a world of sweetness to me have the lisping accents had
Since the day those lips so rosy learned to softly whisper "Dad,"
And we thought it truly wondrous in a babe whose months were nine,
And that no smarter child existed than that little girl of mine.

Now a whispered consultation, then she climbs upon my knee,
And tells me that they'd like to play at hide-and-seek with me.
How vainly do I strive to tell her no and raise a frown!
But her comrades join her pleading, and I lay my old pipe down,

And rise up from my rocker, and responsive to their
    call,
Soon I'm playing "fait" and "catcher," and the wildest
    of them all;
Yet I don't regret the comfort that she forced me to re-
    sign,
As I chase the flying footsteps of that little girl of mine.

Now the children all are going; it is getting late, I
    think;
The curly head is nodding and the eyes begin to blink.
For upon his nightly mission the old sandman starts to
    creep,
To visit all the babies and send them off to sleep.
So I press her to my bosom, as she softly says "good-
    night,"
And place her, locked in slumber, in the bed so clean
    and white;
And I even kiss the mattress where the rounded limbs
    recline,
And invoke the care of angels o'er that little girl of
    mine.

And when old Time has speeded, and I near the close of
    life,
And my little daughter's grown into a mother and a
    wife,
As I sit around her fireside, with her children at my
    knee,
And tell them what a comfort their dear mother was to
    me,
Though her features are mature and her form of youth-
    ful grace
Has grown to stately womanhood, yet memory will ef-
    face
The lengthy intervening years, and my fond thoughts
    will incline
To the days when all I called her was that little girl of
    mine.

TO LUCILE.

My little girl is lying
   Upon her pillow white,
With angels round her flying,
   Though hid from mortal sight.
One hand, with outstretched finger,
   Lies softly on her breast,
As lovingly I linger
   O'er my darling in her nest.

The smiles are running riot
   Across the rosy face,
That knows no hour of quiet
   Throughout the daylight's space;
While now and them comes fleeting
   A look so glad, it seems
As if she hears the greeting
   Of angels in her dreams.

The eyes that in the daytime
   Are never filled with tears,
That sparkle through the playtime
   Which with the morn appears,
Are closed in tired sleeping,
   Which knows no halt or break,
Until the dawn comes creeping
   To bid my love awake.

May heaven let me keep her
   Until these locks are gray!
And may the ruthless reaper
   For years remain away!
May some among the number
   Of cherubs round God's shrine,
Always watch o'er her slumber,
   This little girl of mine!

THE RIVER.

(Written during the high water of 1897.)

With a rush and a roar, in a furious wrath,
    Comes the King of American rivers;
Great God! what a terrible power he hath!
See, see, as he travels his widening path,
    How the countryside trembles and quivers!

See, see, the fair towns that he met on his way,
    How he hath in his meshes entwined them!
As he cometh adown in his fearful array,
"Woe, woe!" in his anger he seemeth to say,
    "To your levees and all that's behind them!"

Hear the sweep and the swirl of his gigantic force,
    That at times is so placid and listless!
A giant is he at his uttermost source,
And the strength that he gains on his torrent-like
      course
    To the Gulf, makes him well nigh resistless.

See the ruin he wrought as he angrily tore
    From the line where he joins with Missouri!
See the wrecks that bestrew Mississippi's fair shore!
See the Arkansas farms that are smiling no more,
    Since the tyrant came down in his fury!

Hear the wild battle songs that ring out to the skies
    From the forces that follow his banner!
In their devilish laughter and demon-like cries,
With a world of foreboding and threatening lies
    'Gainst the peace of our own Louisiana!

But let's drive off the fear that our bosoms makes cold,
    As we gaze on the foeman so royal!
Let us work and assist our brave levees to hold,
For we'll win in the fight 'gainst this enemy bold,
    If we only are watchful and loyal.

CONCEIT.

I do hate a man that's conceited, a fellow whose mind
    is inflated
With a sense of his own self-importance, who firmly
    thinks he's elevated
Above other mortals around him, in some certain par-
    ticular feature,
And than whom I am of the opinion there's no more in-
    sufferable creature.

Of course, every man should be proud of, for instance,
    a noble ancestry,
Of fathers whose names were illustrious in field or in
    senate, or vestry,
Or he should, if his merit's unusual and he's gained the
    world's noticing by it,
Take pride in his worthy achievements—and I'd be the
    last to decry it.

But that's not the point I am making, which is this:
    There's a strong demarcation
'Twixt conceit, which is truly disgusting, and a proper
    self-appreciation;
The one is the gift of Jehovah, the other the devil cre-
    ated—
And pride makes a fellow respected, while conceit
    causes him to be hated.

And the worst form of all is the purse pride! By the
    heavens, I think I would rather
Break rocks than be rich if it caused me to think that
    because my respected old father
Had made for his offspring a fortune, by dint of his
    shrewdness and labor,
I'm too great to bestow recognition on my poorer,
    though just as good neighbor.

That's it; there are hundreds of people whose wealth
   reaches five or six figures,
And whose intellectual development is about on a par
   with a Digger's,
Who have naught in the world to their credit save the
   gold their old dads did bequeath 'em,
And who pass the old fellow, their master in mind, as if
   poverty made him beneath 'em.

And all hail to the shining exceptions—those men of a
   gen'rous expansion,
Who shun not the poor man who lives in a cot, while
   they pass their lives in a mansion.
And who, because clerks work for wages, don't think
   they're removed far above 'em,
All hail to these democrats with a small d—and I wish
   there were many more of 'em.

He was wise who declared that honor and fame arise
   not from any condition,
The question should be what's your merit, and not your
   financial position!
A knave and a fool may be born in a home 'mid sur-
   roundings rich, 'ristocratic,
While honesty and genius may first see the light within
   the confines of an attic.

And, again, ye rich churls, I would ask you, in the eyes
   of the Ruler of heaven,
Think ye ye're the whitest of flour, while the poor man's
   considered the leaven?
By the Lord, it may be when they've gone from this
   world of exchanges and barter,
They'll emulate Dives' example and ask Lazarus for
   one drop of water.

Yes, you're right, Thomas Hood, in bemoaning in mel-
    lifluous verses the rarity
On earth of the God-given attribute, of which mortals
    have knowledge as charity,
And which, had it wider dominion, would lessen the
    world's discontentment,
And obviate, 'gainst the proud man's contumely, his
    poor neighbor's natural resentment.

As for me, I have one creed to go by; 'tis this, without
    prologue or sequel,
I don't think our Maker intended that men be created
    unequal,
Or that He drew a line of distinction 'twixt this, that, or
    t'other earth resident;
And the honest man on a car is as good as I am—and
    I'm just as good as the President.

THE LAY OF THE CIGARETTE.

Hurrah, hurrah, for yours tru-lee,
    For I'm the cigarette!
I've killed many millions un-du-lee,
    And will kill many more, you bet.
Go search the churchyard, grave by grave,
    Where the weird ghouls congregate;
Each second hole contains my slave,
    And my victim, soon or late.

Go ask the un-der-ta-ki-er,
        Now grown so rich and proud,
Or the festive coffin ma-ki-er,
        Or the man who sews the shroud—
Go ask them all who most supplies
        The fortunes large they get,
And hear each one as he loudly cries,
        "The deadly cigarette."

Just gaze on the dudelet, wan-der-ing,
        With less brains than a fly,
But don't waste time in pon-der-ing
        Who made him so—'twas I.
Go seek madhouses everywhere,
        Those dens of misery,
And count the thousands gibbering there,
        Who owe their fate to me.

Grim war, whom fools call glo-ri-ous,
        And cholera, swift and sly,
Have neither been vic-to-ri-ous
        Over more victims than I.
Among my slaves are young and old,
        The outcast and the pet;
There are few who 'scape the fatal hold
        Of the deadly cigarette.

Then a three times three, right mer-ri-ly,
        And a three times three again,
For one who's lost, yea, ver-i-ly,
        The count of his victims slain;
Who numbers slaves in every land,
        Where the sun doth rise or set,
Who's justly styled grim Death's right hand,
        The deadly cigarette.

INTO THE FUTURE.

I take my baby from the floor and place him on my
 knee,
And wonder, as I stroke his hair, exactly what he'll be;
And I ask the ancient sybil who guards the future dim,
To show unto mine eyes the fate she holds in store for
 him.

But receiving not an answer from the crone so old and
 wise,
I strive to read the future in his blue and liquid eyes,
And I seek to find out whether his path in coming years
Will lead him o'er the mount of joy or through the vale
 of tears.

Is he going to be a doctor?   Will lips that raved with
 pain
Beseech God's blessings on his head for bringing health
 again?
Will woman's soft and tender eyes with grateful tears
 grow dim,
Because of husband, brother, child, made well and
 strong through him?

Or will he be a warrior?   Will on the battlefield
His voice be raised in thunder tone to bid the foeman
 yield?
And if such prove his future, on which side will he be?
Will his arm back a tyrant's will, or strive for liberty?

Or will he turn to science? Will those two shining eyes
Discover unknown planets in the heaven's spreading
 skies?
Or will some new invention that benefits mankind
Acknowledge as its author the genius of his mind?

Or will he be a lawyer, learned in his country's laws,
To plead in courts of justice some worthy client's
     cause?
And will the robes of ermine one day enwrap the form
That now I hold so tightly in the shelter of my arm?

Will he become a statesman and let words of wisdom
     fall,
As he pleads for right and justice in the legislative hall,
And, dying, leave behind him a great and noble fame,
That ages to come after may glorify his name?

Will he make Art his mistress, and put Millais to the
     blush,
While Titian pales beside him as beside the sun the
     rush?
Or will he as a poet sing till Byron's voice grows dumb,
And Burns' name is heard no more, in the changing
     years to come?

Or will he be a searcher into Nature's wondrous laws
And with undying Newton claim the grateful world's
     applause?
Or will earth-famous books spring forth from 'neath
     his flowing pen,
To bring far nobler, purer thoughts unto the minds of
     men?

Will he become an actor, and in passioned tones de-
     claim,
While thousands crowd to see the man who rivals Irv-
     ing's fame?
Or have the fates decreed for him a mediocre life—
His home his stage, his plaudits but from children and
     from wife?

Or—here my thoughts grow anxious, and I scarce re-
      press the sigh—
Will he become a libertine, or as a drunkard die?
Or will he as a gambler entwine the fatal loop
Around the head and bosom of some unsuspecting
      dupe?

Nay, God forbid!   And may He some angel deputize
To guard my infant's onward steps with ever-watchful
      eyes;
And, whatever path He wills my boy in life's fast fleet-
      ing span,
I pray that He may make of him a good and honest
      man.

————

THE PATENT UNBREAKABLE DOLL.

On the day that our daughter was five years old,
  We thought we'd endeavor to get,
If we could, 'mongst the things that the toydealers sold,
  Some plaything she hadn't as yet.
The search appeared vain, as we ransacked, that morn,
  Every store at which we made a call,
Till in one my wife's quick, eager glances fell on
  A patent unbreakable doll.

The salesman spoke well of the wonderful toy,
  And the strength that its sturdy frame had;
So the dolly came home, to our little girl's joy,
  While our youngest, a two-year-old lad,
As a sneer to his features did fervently cling,
  Seemed thinking, "What fools are you all!
Just give me a chance, and I won't do a thing
  To your patent unbreakable doll."

Next day came his chance; in a casual way
   He gouged out the dolly's left eye;
Then a twist of his hand, and before you could say
   "Jack Robinson," an arm was awry;
With a critical grin, he pulled off the nose;
   A jerk, and the right ear did fall;
'Twas the work of a second to knock off the toes
   Of that patent unbreakable doll.

And his brow was as calm as a soft summer night,
   While his eyes had the satisfied glow
Of the soldier who conquers and puts to the flight
   His so-called invincible foe.
Wife and I just then came in at the door;
   There he stood, like Napoleon of Gaul,
Midst the wreck and the ruin that cumbered the floor,
   From that patent unbreakable doll.

So we looked at each other with quivering lip,
   And the thought round each bosom did coil,
That we'd give up our long-planned Egyptian trip,
   For we wished no international broil,
And we feared, if the eyes of that vandal-like kid
   On the pyramids happened to fall,
He'd perchance serve old Cheops the same way he did
   That patent unbreakable doll.

THE MAIDEN'S DECISION.

Jack's Letter—

"I offer you an humble lot,
A cozy, vine-embowered cot,
A home where luxury is not,
    But where, sweet elf,
No grim despair or sorrow black
Will ever cross your young life's track,
Where love shall recompense the lack
    Of worldly pelf."

Bullion's Letter—

"I offer you my hoarded store,
Fine dresses, jewels, wealth galore,
A carriage and a coach-and-four
    In which to ride;
A brownstone mansion on the Row,
A life of glittering ease and show,
And joys that you will never know,
    Save as my bride."

The Maid—

"I really don't know how to choose;
I don't want handsome Jack to lose,
Nor yet old Bullion's wealth refuse—
    O, saints above!
With Jack to poverty I'm tied,
While if I be old Bullion's bride,
My wildest dreams are satisfied—
    Yet Jack I love!

But, ah! I think I see a way:
I'll Bullion wed; he's old and gray,
And with his fathers soon must lay,
    Then I'll wear black,
A widow be with lots of gold,
And when the year of mourning's told,
I do not think I'll be too old
    To marry Jack."

WERE I A WOMAN.

Were I a woman, meek or gay, when men in crowded
    cars should say:
"Take this seat, miss (or 'ma'am), I pray,"
I would not take the proffered seat, unless I'd say, as
    would be meet,
"I thank you, sir," in accents sweet,
        Were I a woman!

Were I a woman, I would shun to leave my household
    work undone,
While to the matinee I'd run;
I'd not in mornings lie awake, and needless time in
    dressing take,
Nor breakfast force my hub to make,
        Were I a woman!

Were I a woman, dainty, rare, I'd not invite, on thor-
    oughfare,
The idle lounger's wanton stare;
I'd not up to Canal street wend each day and bargain
    sales attend,
My husband's hard-earned pelf to spend,
        Were I a woman!

Were I a woman, I would scorn to gad around from
    early morn
Until the sun to rest had gone;
Nor would I scandalously rend to pieces name of absent
    friend,
But stoutly would her fame defend,
        Were I a woman!

Were I a woman, I'd not like in pants an uncouth pose
    to strike,
And show my figure on a bike;
A woman true I'd strive to be, and this "new woman"
    heresy
Would never make a slave of me,
        Were I a woman!

THE NEW ORLEANS GIRL.

Other bards may indite their verse to the night,
　Or the waves dashing high on the coast,
May chant forth their lays to the soft summer days,
　Or to battles of host against host;
To the flowers and trees, or the spring's balmy breeze,
　Or to brooks that through forest scenes purl—
But far higher my theme is, far sweeter my dream is;
　For I sing of the New Orleans girl.

Both as sweetheart and wife, all the troubles of life
　Are softened and eased at her touch, 　　.
And with her by our side we care not what betide,
　We laugh at grim Poverty's clutch.
Be her eyes black or brown, or the bluest in town,
　Be her hair in a braid or a curl,
Whate'er be her name, she is always the same—
　Our idol, the New Orleans girl.

No form is more neat, no lips are more sweet,
　No eyes than her own are more bright;
No heart is more loyal, no manner more royal,
　No spirits than hers are more light.
One glance of her eye, soft as moon in the sky,
　Sets the hearts of her lovers awhirl,
And there's none upon earth who'd not give all his
　　worth
　For the love of the New Orleans girl.

The gay demoiselle of whom French gallants tell,
　The fraulein of Germany's shore,
The canny Scot's pride and the Irishman's bride,
　The maid whom the English adore;
All are charming, I ween, but before our fair queen
　Their banners of beauty must furl,
As we fondly caress her, we murmur "God bless her
　Forever—the New Orleans girl."

www.ingramcontent.com/pod-product-compliance
Lightning Source LLC
Chambersburg PA
CBHW032249080426
42735CB00008B/1063